# Psalms Of A Remnant Woman

## Volume I

Nina Barnett

BookLeaf
Publishing

India | USA | UK

Made with ❤ on the BookLeaf Publishing Platform
www.bookleafpub.in
www.bookleafpub.com

# Dedication

*My heart is overflowing with a good theme;*
*I recite my composition concerning the King;*
*My tongue is the pen of a ready writer.*


**Psalm 45:1 NKJV**

# Preface

I'll tell you who the remnant woman is. She's you. She's me. She's the women who are close to us and those who are simply passersby. The remnant woman is a woman who has been tried by fire but has not been consumed. She has walked through valleys, faced storms, and encountered countless adversities, yet she emerges with her faith intact, her heart surrendered, and her spirit victorious. The poems in this collection are not mere words but the cries, prayers, and praises of a woman who has learned what it means to truly live for Christ.

These **Psalms of a Remnant Woman** are not born in moments of ease, but in the depths—where surrender met struggle, where pain was overshadowed by divine purpose, and where victory was realized through worship. The remnant woman is not just a survivor; she is a soldier, chosen and called for such a time as this. She stands in the gap for her family, her community, and her generation, clothed in the armor of God and the authority of the One who has called her.

This collection of poems is my heart poured out to every woman who feels hidden, forgotten, ostracized, abandoned, rejected, misjudged, mistreated, and overlooked. You are not alone. Like the women of old who carried the weight of their faith with unshakable courage, we, too, rise with holy boldness. These psalms are the anthem of every woman who chooses to live not by the world's standards but by the Word of God. As you read, may you find your voice, strength, and divine calling echoed in these pages. Remnant woman, arise.

# Acknowledgements

As I reflect on my journey, I am overwhelmed with gratitude for the multitude of individuals who have touched my life and supported me along the way. If I were to acknowledge every single person who has prayed for me, listened to me, wiped my tears, and reminded me of the purpose God has for me, I would need at least ten more pages! To each of you, I extend my heartfelt thanks.

However, there are a few remarkable women whose impact deserves special recognition:

To the remnant woman who inspires my ministry of motherhood, my daughter, *Danae*: God crafted a masterpiece when He created you. You embody the finest parts of my spirit, and I eagerly anticipate watching you flourish in this vast world. Remember, you can do all things through Christ who strengthens you. His promises are steadfast regarding your life, and I will live to see them come to pass.

To the remnant woman who brought me into this world, my mother, *Mrs. Eunice Barnett*: I can only imagine the challenges you faced giving birth to me prematurely and watching my tiny body struggle to breathe. Your faith fought for me before I had the strength to fight for myself. I am grateful for you, and I am proud to call you my mother.

To my sister, *Sheena Turner*, who shares the same womb as I do: You are powerful and bold in your own right. Thank you for being the shoulder I needed to cry on and the ear I required during moments of frustration. You have been a refuge for me on countless occasions.

To my spiritual mother, *Apostle Natrietia McClendon*, who birthed me in the Spirit: Thank you for doing life with me and for seeing in me what I often could not see myself. Your gentle, firm hand has pushed me from the nest, in the most loving way, assuring me that I would always have a safe place to land.

To *Mrs. Andrea Williams*, my sister in spirit who has journeyed with me toward healing and purpose: What can I say? We have crossed the gun line together. This has been a long journey, but I wouldn't change a single moment of it.

To all the remnant women who have shaped my path, your love and support have been invaluable, and I am eternally grateful.

# 1. A Premature Arrival

Out of the womb, before my time,
I was born, breathless and silent,
The world awaited my cry, but none came,
For my lungs were frail, and my ears were closed.

Yet, You, my Lord, were there in the stillness,
The whisper of life hovered over me,
As I struggled to grasp what others took with ease.
I could not hear the sounds of creation,
But I knew the voice of my Creator.

The dragon stood, waiting to devour me,
But the hand of the Almighty One shielded me.
I was weak in the eyes of men,
Yet strong in the plan of God.
I was small, yet You called me mighty,
Anointed from birth to carry Your name.

Though the breath in my chest was shallow,
Your ruach filled me with life everlasting.
Though my ears were deaf to the world,
My heart heard the rhythm of heaven.

You set me apart from the moment of my arrival,

For Your word was sealed upon my soul.
The enemy sought to destroy me,
But Your command held him back,
For I am Your remnant,
Chosen before I could speak,
Appointed before I could walk.

My weakness was my strength in You,
For the breath I could not muster, You breathed for me.
The song I could not hear, You sang over me.
Though I entered the world frail and feeble,
I rise now in Your power and Your purpose.

The dragon rages, but I fear not,
For the woman clothed in the sun is my heritage,
Her offspring, those who keep Your commandments,
And hold fast to the testimony of Jesus.

I stand in the shelter of Your wings,
A remnant, born early, yet born for this hour,
To declare Your praise in the land of the living,
To overcome by the blood of the Lamb
And the word of my testimony.

Let all who see me know
I am not the work of human hands,
But the craftsmanship of the King of Kings.

Though the enemy sought to claim me,
I was born for such a time as this.

Hallelujah!
The remnant woman lives.

# 2. Wounds Beneath the Bloodline

How long will I carry this weight?
The burden of blood and the ties that bind,
For in my own house I have found no rest,
And among those who should lift me, I have known pain.
The voices of elders speak not of wisdom,
But of wounds, their words heavy with judgment,
Their hands raised not in blessing, but in control,
And I, the remnant, stand alone in the storm.

I sought refuge in the arms of family,
Yet their embrace has been cold,
A cloak of tradition that suffocates the soul.
Their eyes see only their ways,
And their hearts have hardened to my cries.
They say, "This is how it must be,"
But Your Spirit, my Lord, whispers another way.
You are not the God of chains,
But the God of freedom and truth.

Lord, hear my cry!
For I have honored them as You have commanded,
Yet their yoke is heavy,
And their judgment fierce.

They claim to know You,
But their ways are far from Your heart.
In their midst, I am silenced,
My voice but a whisper in a room full of thunder.

They see not the call You've placed upon me,
Nor the anointing You've poured upon my head.
I am but a daughter in their eyes,
A vessel for their plans,
Yet You have called me for more,
For greater things than their words can hold.
They dismiss what they do not understand,
But You, my God, know the truth that burns within.

How long, my Lord, will I endure this trial?
How long will the hands of those who should guide
Instead tear at my spirit,
And speak words that wound?
But You, my God, are my defender,
My shield against the arrows of the heart.
You see the hidden wounds,
The scars that no one else knows,
And You will heal what others have broken.

I trust You,
For You are the lifter of my head.
Though family may forsake me,

You will never leave me.
Though elders may misunderstand,
You know the path You've set before me.
In Your arms, I find my rest,
And in Your voice, I hear my calling.

O remnant woman, rise from the ashes of their words,
For your worth is not in their approval,
But in the love of the Father who called you His own.
Walk boldly, even in the midst of their disdain,
For the Lord has anointed you,
And His plan for you will not fail.
The chains of tradition cannot bind what God has set
free,
And the voices of the past will not silence His call.

I will wait on You, my Lord,
And in Your time, You will make all things right.
Until then, I will stand,
Unmoved by their expectations,
And faithful to Your voice alone.

# 3. Whispers in the Dark

Lord, You saw me in the darkness,
When shadows became my dwelling place,
And the hands that should have held me in love
Struck me with violence instead.

Behind closed doors, I was broken,
Each bruise a whisper of my worthlessness,
Each blow a lie I began to believe.
I cried out in silence,
But my voice was lost in the storm of fear,
Trapped in a prison built of pain.

Yet even there, my God,
You heard the whispers in the dark.
You saw the tears I could not show the world,
And Your heart was moved by my suffering.

You, my Lord, are my Deliverer.
When I could not escape, You came for me.
When I thought the darkness would swallow me whole,
Your light broke through like dawn.

You held me when no one else would,
You whispered words of truth over the lies.

"I am with you," You said,
"Do not be afraid, for I will never leave you."

Though my body was bruised,
You shielded my spirit,
Though my soul was torn,
You mended me with love.

I am not the sum of my suffering,
For You have called me by name.
I am not defined by the violence done to me,
But by the grace that has restored me.

Now I stand, no longer in chains,
For Your mercy has set me free.
The darkness has no claim on me,
For Your light shines brighter still.

The whispers of fear have faded,
Replaced by Your voice of truth,
Saying, "You are mine,
And no one can snatch you from My hand."

My Lord, my Redeemer,
You have made beauty rise from my ashes.
What was meant to destroy me
Has become a testimony of Your power.

I will praise You,
For I have survived what sought to break me.
I will declare Your faithfulness,
For You brought me out of the shadows
Into the glorious light of Your love.

You, my God, are my refuge,
And though I carry the scars of the past,
They now shine as marks of Your deliverance,
Proof that I am not forsaken,
But forever held in Your hands.

The darkness has passed,
And I stand,
Whole in Your light.

# 4. Choices Carried

Lord, You know the weight I bear,
The burden of choices made in the shadows,
When fear clouded my heart,
And silence screamed louder than my faith.

In that moment, I stumbled,
Gripped by shame and confusion,
I chose a path I now grieve,
A road of regret paved with tears.

But You, my God, did not turn away.
In my darkest hour, when guilt suffocated me,
You came close,
Not with condemnation,
But with mercy unmeasured,
And love that has no bounds.

I carried my choice like a heavy stone,
The secret shame that broke me from within.
Yet You, my Lord,
Carried me.

When I could not stand, You lifted me.
When I could not forgive myself,

Your forgiveness washed over me like rain,
Cleansing every wound I thought would never heal.

You are the God who redeems what is lost,
Who restores what is broken.
In my ashes, You placed beauty,
In my sorrow, You spoke hope.

Though my hands once carried the weight of regret,
You placed a new song in my heart,
A song of grace,
A song of life reborn through Your love.

I am not bound by my past,
For You have set me free.
I am not condemned by my choices,
For Your blood speaks a better word.

Now I stand, redeemed by Your mercy,
Forgiven by Your endless grace.
What I carried in guilt,
You now carry in Your arms of love,
And the weight has lifted,
For in You, I am made whole.

My God, my Lord, my Redeemer,
I will sing of Your faithfulness,

For You have turned my mourning into joy,
And my brokenness into beauty.

Let my life be a testimony,
Of a choice once carried in pain,
But now carried in grace,
Redeemed by the One
Who makes all things new.

# 5. Perfection's Weight

My Lord, You know my heart,
How I've labored beneath the weight of perfection,
Chasing a standard I could never reach,
A measure I could never fill.
Day and night, I toiled,
Wearing myself thin,
Believing that flawlessness
Would bring me closer to You.

I sought to build a life without cracks,
A heart without blemish,
Yet every effort left me shattered,
Every failure a reminder of my frailty.
The more I strove,
The farther You seemed,
As if my striving built a wall
Between Your grace and my weary soul.

I longed to be without fault,
But my hands are dust,
And my heart—so fragile—
Could not bear the burden I placed upon it.

Yet You, my God,

Are not the God who demands perfection,
But the One who perfects.
You do not ask for flawlessness,
But for surrender.

You whispered to me in my striving,
"Be still and know that I am God."
You saw the cracks I tried to hide,
The wounds I tried to mend alone.
Yet it was in my brokenness
That You drew near,
Not with rebuke,
But with mercy overflowing.

I was not created to carry the weight of perfection,
For You alone are perfect.
And in Your grace, You make me whole,
Not by my own doing,
But by Your love that covers all.

Now I see, my Lord,
That You desire not my perfection,
But my trust.
You ask not for flawlessness,
But for a heart willing to be molded,
A vessel, though cracked,
Through which Your glory shines.

My Lord, my strength and my refuge,
I lay down this burden before You,
The need to perform,
The fear of failing.
For in Your presence, I am enough,
Not because of what I do,
But because of who You are.

You are the God who works through weakness,
Who brings beauty from brokenness.
And now, I stand,
Not perfect,
But redeemed,
Not flawless,
But held in the hands of the One
Who makes all things new.

Forever, I will praise You,
For Your grace is my sufficiency.
You are my perfection,
My righteousness,
My all in all.

I rest in You,
And find peace beyond my striving,

For in Your love,
I am made whole.

# 6. A Silent Strain

You see the struggle that grips my soul,
The battle fought in secret, beneath the weight of this
burden.
I cry out to You in my weakness,
For the chains of this addiction hold me fast.
These pills I once trusted for relief
Now bind me like a prisoner in a foreign land.

I sought comfort, O God,
In the quiet of my pain,
Turning to what numbed the ache,
Yet the very thing that promised peace
Has taken me captive.
I hide in the shadows,
Afraid to be seen,
Ashamed of my dependence,
But You, my Lord, know it all.

You see the tears I weep in silence,
The moments when the bottle calls louder than Your
voice.
How many times have I promised to stop?
How many days have I sworn this would be the last?
But the grip is strong,

And I am weary of the fight.

Yet still, You remain,
Unshaken by my failures,
Unmoved by my shame.
Your mercy, like a river, flows to me,
Even here, where the chains tighten around my soul.

God, I long to be free,
To walk again in the light of Your promise,
But the weight of this battle is heavy,
And I am so very weak.
Still, You whisper to me in the darkness,
"Come to Me, all who are weary, and I will give you rest."

You are the only One who can break these chains,
The only One who can lift the weight from my soul.
I have tried on my own, and failed,
But You, my Lord, are my Deliverer.

So I lift my hands to You,
Even in my brokenness,
Even in my shame.
For I know that You are greater than this struggle,
Your power stronger than this addiction.
You, my God, can restore what has been lost,
Heal what has been broken,

And breathe life into what feels dead inside me.

My Lord, do not forsake me in this place,
For I cannot break free on my own.
But I believe in Your promise,
That where the Spirit of the Lord is,
There is freedom.

Come, Lord, with Your mighty hand,
Break the chains that bind me,
Lift the weight from my soul.
For I long to walk in the light once more,
Redeemed by Your grace,
And freed by Your power.

Even in this struggle, I will trust You,
For You are faithful,
And Your love endures forever.
You are my strength in weakness,
My hope in despair,
My freedom in captivity.

# 7. Abandonment Echoes

Lord, hear my cry in the stillness of night,
For the echoes of abandonment surround me,
Like shadows that whisper in the silence.
Where is the hand that once held mine?
Where is the voice that once called me beloved?
They have turned and gone,
Leaving me alone in the wilderness of my heart.

My soul feels the weight of desertion,
Like a tree uprooted, cast aside by the winds.
I look for comfort,
But none is near,
I seek refuge,
But the walls around me crumble.
God, do You see the ache within me?
Do You hear the cry no one else hears?

They left me, my Lord,
Like a stranger passing by,
And I am left with the void,
A silence that speaks louder than words.
Yet even in the loneliness,
I turn to You, my King,
For You are the One who never leaves,

The One who never forsakes.

Though the echoes of abandonment ring in my ears,
Your voice cuts through the noise.
You call me by name,
A name I thought was forgotten.
You draw near to me,
Closer than any human heart could.
Where others turned away,
You remain.

O God, You are my refuge in this storm,
The shelter in my desolation.
I thought I was forsaken,
But in the depths of my sorrow,
I find You waiting,
With arms open wide.

The void left by those who abandoned me,
You fill with Your presence.
The tears that fall in the quiet,
You catch and turn to joy.
For though man may forsake,
You, my Lord, are steadfast,
Unshaken by my fears,
Unmoved by my doubts.

Even in the echo of abandonment,
I find Your love resounding.
What was broken, You restore,
What was lost, You redeem.
You are the Father to the fatherless,
The Friend to the friendless,
The God who sees me
When no one else does.

So I will rest in You, O Lord,
Though the world may turn away,
You are my anchor,
My strong tower.
Let the echoes fade into silence,
For Your voice is the one I will follow,
And Your love is the one I will trust.

You, my God, have not abandoned me,
And in Your presence, I am found.

# 8. Found

Lord, I wandered as one forsaken,
A child without a father's hand to guide,
No voice to calm my fears, no arms to hold me.
In the silence, I cried out to You,
In the emptiness, I longed for a love unknown.

I sought for peace in barren places,
For shelter in the shadows of my pain,
But none could fill the void within,
None could heal the wound of absence.

Yet in my wandering, You found me, Abba,
You, the Father of the fatherless,
Called me by name and claimed me as Your own.
When others turned away,
You drew near,
When I was forgotten,
You remembered me.

Your love, my Lord, is deeper than my need,
For where my heart was hollow,
You filled it with Your grace.
Where my soul was fractured,
You bound it with Your mercy.

You are the Father I have always longed for,
The One who never leaves,
The One who never fails.

In Your arms, I found my rest,
In Your presence, I found my peace.
No longer am I lost or abandoned,
For You have claimed me as Your daughter,
And in Your house, I have a place.

You have restored what was taken from me,
Rebuilt what was broken in me,
And now I stand, fatherless no more,
But found,
Found in the love of a Father
Whose faithfulness knows no end.

My Lord, I will praise You all my days,
For in Your care, I have been made whole.
You, my refuge,
You, my Father,
You, my eternal home.

# 9. Who am I?

Who am I, O Lord?
For I stand as a stranger to myself,
Tossed by the winds of confusion,
Pulled by the tides of doubt.
The face I see in the mirror is unfamiliar,
A reflection blurred by the weight of questions.
Am I the daughter You have called,
Or the wanderer lost in her own name?

I have searched for myself in the eyes of others,
Only to find empty stares and hollow words.
I have chased the world's labels,
Wearing their judgments like garments,
Yet none fit the soul You have formed in me.
My heart longs to know its true shape,
But the voices of the world shout louder than Your
whispers.

Who am I, O God,
When I feel torn between who I was
And who I am meant to be?
I wear masks to hide the fragments of my soul,
Yet even behind them, I feel exposed.
The weight of expectation presses upon me,

And the more I strive, the less I recognize myself.

Yet in the quiet, You call me.
You speak to the deepest places,
To the heart confused and wandering.
You remind me that I am Yours—
Not defined by the labels of this world,
Nor by the wounds of my past.
You, O Lord, have named me before time began,
Your design written on my very soul.

Who am I but the one You have redeemed?
Who am I but the child of Your love?
When I search for myself in the world,
I come up empty.
But when I look to You,
I find the identity I have long sought.
You are my Creator,
And in You, I am made whole.

I am not what the world says I am,
Nor what the past has shaped me to be.
I am who You declare me to be, O Lord,
Chosen, beloved, called by name.
Though I wrestle with doubt,
Your truth anchors me.
Though I falter in my steps,

Your grace guides me home.

So, I surrender my search,
And rest in the name You have given me.
For You alone know who I am,
And in You, I find my true self.
I am Yours, O Lord,
And that is enough.

No longer will I wander,
For in Your presence, I am found.
No longer will I question,
For Your love is my answer.
Who am I, O God?
I am the remnant woman,
Known and loved by You.

# 10. What You Speak Over Me

O Lord, I stand before You,
Trembling beneath the weight of Your words,
For You have spoken over me what I could not say
myself.
You call me beloved,
Yet I have seen myself as broken.
You name me chosen,
While I have wandered, lost and forgotten.
You declare me whole,
Even when I see only the scars of my past.

Who am I, O Lord, that You would speak such things?
For the world has given me names I wear like chains,
And my heart, frail and unsure,
Has believed the lies of my past.
But You, O God, have called me out of the shadows,
And in Your voice, I find a truth I cannot deny.

You say I am fearfully and wonderfully made,
When all I see is weakness and failure.
You declare me righteous,
When I struggle to forgive myself for my sin.
You call me Your daughter,

Even when I feel unworthy to stand in Your presence.

O Lord, how can I doubt Your words
When they are life to my weary soul?
You have breathed identity into my spirit,
And Your truth cuts through the lies I believed.
You say I am more than a conqueror,
Though my feet have stumbled, and my hands are
scarred.
You speak of victory,
When all I've known are battles I thought I'd lost.

But now, O God, I choose to believe.
I take hold of what You say,
For Your words are higher than mine,
And Your truth stands eternal.
The world may see one thing,
But You see the masterpiece You've created,
Formed in Your image,
Crafted by Your hand.

I am who You say I am—
No longer defined by the weight of my past,
Nor by the opinions of men.
I will walk in the name You have given me,
For Your voice is the only one I will follow.
Your Word is my anchor,

Your promises my guide.

You have called me victorious,
And so I will stand in Your strength.
You have named me loved,
And so I will rest in Your embrace.
What You say, O Lord,
Is what I will believe.

No longer will I doubt,
No longer will I turn away.
I am Yours, O God,
And I will walk boldly in Your truth.
For what You speak over me,
Is the only word that will remain.

# 11. Made

O Lord, You have known me from the depths,
Woven in secret by Your hand,
Crafted in the quiet places of Your heart.
Before I spoke my first breath, You called me forth,
And in Your sight, I was formed,
Fearfully and wonderfully made.

Who am I, that You would create me so?
For I have seen my flaws,
Felt the weight of imperfection,
But Your hands have traced each line of my being,
Every detail—
You call it beautiful.

The world may measure me by its standards,
But You, O God, measure by love.
In my weakness, You see strength,
In my frailty, You see design.
You shaped me with purpose,
Each scar, each bruise,
A testimony of Your grace.

O Lord, You have made me whole,
Even when I have seen myself as broken.

When I stand in the mirror,
You stand beside me,
Speaking truth to every doubt,
Telling me I am more than what the world says.

I will no longer hide, O God,
For Your hands have worked wonders in me.
Every inch of my being,
Every thought in my mind—
It is known by You,
And You have called it good.

Fearfully and wonderfully made,
This is my name, O Lord.
I am not an accident,
Nor a mistake,
But the masterpiece of Your imagination,
Breathed into life by Your Spirit.

You have numbered my days,
And I am precious in Your sight.
The plans You have for me are vast,
And I stand amazed at Your wisdom.
Even when I falter,
You remind me of who I am—
Yours, beloved, known before time.

So I will walk in this truth, O God,
Knowing I am crafted by Your hand.
No more will I despise what You have made,
For I am fearfully,
And wonderfully made.

Let my soul sing of Your goodness,
For I am a reflection of Your love.
In Your eyes, I am whole,
And in Your arms, I am complete.
This is my truth, O Lord,
Forever I am fearfully and wonderfully made.

# 12. From the Depths I Rise

O Lord, from the depths I called out to You,
When the weight of life crushed my soul,
And the shadows swallowed all my light.
In that darkest hour, I sought escape,
Believing the lie that silence would bring peace.

The night was heavy upon me,
The abyss beneath me opened wide.
My heart was shattered,
My spirit crushed under the burden of despair.
I saw no way forward,
And in my pain, I thought the end was all I had left.

But You, O God, did not turn away.
When I let go of life, You held fast to me.
Your mercy reached into the pit,
Your love caught me in the fall.

In the silence where I thought I'd be forgotten,
You whispered my name,
And Your voice pulled me from the brink.

You, O Lord, are the God of the broken,
The One who heals the deepest wounds.

Even in the valley of death, You were there,
Your hand lifted me from the grave
And breathed life into my weary bones.

You saw my despair,
Yet You did not let it define me.
Where I saw an end,
You spoke a beginning.
Where I saw only ashes,
You made beauty rise.

I stand now, O God,
Not because of my strength,
But because of Your grace.
You have brought me back from the edge,
And in Your presence, I have found hope again.

I wear no shame,
For You have turned my mourning into joy.
I carry no guilt,
For Your mercy covers me like a shield.

I thought I was beyond redemption,
But You are the God who redeems all things.
You have lifted me from the depths
And set my feet upon solid ground.

I will praise You, Lord of my salvation,
For You have saved me from myself.
I will sing of Your faithfulness,
For You were with me when I had lost all hope.

Now, I declare to the weary and broken,
There is no depth too deep for His love.
There is no darkness too dark for His light.
I am living, breathing proof
That His grace is greater than any despair.

O Lord, my Deliverer,
From the depths I rise,
Not by my might,
But by Your hand alone.

I will live to proclaim Your goodness,
For You are the God who saves,
The One who turns sorrow into song,
And death into life.

# 13. Scars that Testify

O Lord, You have seen every wound,
Each mark upon my body,
And the deeper scars unseen by men,
Etched upon my soul.

I once hid them in shame,
Covered the bruises of my past,
For fear that they would tell a story
Of defeat, of brokenness, of failure.

**My scars shall testify!**

But You, O God,
Turned my shame into a testimony.
What was once a sign of pain
Has become a banner of Your faithfulness.

These scars that mar my flesh,
Are now the proof of Your saving hand,
For though I walked through fire,
I was not consumed.
Though I stumbled in the valley,
You lifted me from the pit.

**My scars shall testify!**

I wear them now, these scars,
Not as wounds to be healed
But as marks of Your mercy,
For in every tear, in every ache,
You were there.

When the enemy struck,
You shielded me.
When I was abandoned,
You held me close.
In the depths of despair,
Your light broke through the darkness.

**My scars shall testify!**

Let these scars testify to Your goodness,
For they tell the story not of my suffering,
But of Your deliverance.

What once bled now shines,
With the glory of a heart restored,
A life rebuilt by the hands of my Redeemer.
I am no longer bound by the wounds of my past,
But freed by the grace that carried me through.

**My scars shall testify!**

O Lord, I will sing of Your faithfulness,
For every scar speaks of victory,
Every pain proclaims Your love,
And every tear bears witness
To the God who never leaves nor forsakes His own.

You are faithful, O Lord,
And my scars, once hidden in darkness,
Now shine as testimonies of Your light.

# 14. Breaker of Chains

O Lord, You have seen the chains upon my bloodline,
Generations bound by silent curses,
Sins unspoken but deeply rooted,
Passed down like bitter heirlooms from hand to hand.
Fathers' mistakes became sons' burdens,
Mothers' wounds became daughters' scars.

I have felt the weight of those chains,
Heavy on my soul since birth,
A shadow that walked with me,
A curse that whispered, "You will never be free."

But You, O God, are the God of deliverance,
The One who breaks the iron bars,
Who snaps the cords of oppression
With a single breath of Your power.

You called me forth from the midst of the curse,
Set apart to stand in the gap.
You whispered to me,
"Enough. It ends with you."
And I, trembling but willing,
Rose in faith, trusting Your word.

No longer will the sins of the fathers reign,
No longer will my daughters wear the shame
Of those who came before.
For You, O Lord, have given me the strength
To shatter what has long held us bound.

I lift my voice in warfare,
I lift my hands in surrender,
For I know the battle is not mine,
But Yours.

With every prayer, I break the chains,
With every tear, I water the seeds of freedom.
Generations yet unborn will walk in light,
Because You have anointed me
To walk through the fire
And not be consumed.

The curses once spoken
Fall powerless before Your name,
The patterns of pain dissolve
In the presence of Your glory.
For where there was despair, You planted hope,
Where there was fear, You sowed courage.

I stand now, a remnant woman,
The breaker of chains,

The repairer of the breach.
Through me, You are rewriting the story,
Turning pages soaked in sorrow
Into testimonies of triumph.

My children will know a new legacy,
One not of bondage, but of blessing.
My sons will walk in righteousness,
My daughters will dance in freedom.
For the curse has been broken,
And Your promises endure through every generation.

O Lord, I will praise You with all my breath,
For You have set my bloodline free.
What was once bound in darkness
Now walks in the light of Your truth.

Forever, I will proclaim Your faithfulness,
For You are the God who breaks chains,
The One who delivers from every stronghold.

Generations will rise and call You blessed,
For You have turned the tide,
You have lifted the curse,
And You have called us
To walk in the freedom of Your grace.

# 15. Bruised but Bold

O Lord, You have seen my journey,
The road marked with trials and tears,
Bruises upon my soul from battles fought,
Yet I rise with boldness,
For You are the One who strengthens me.

Though the path has been weary,
And the weight of the world pressed hard against me,
I stand, not by my own might,
But by the power of Your hand.
For You have called me,
And Your call is irrevocable.

Bruised but bold, I step forward,
For I know who goes before me.
The wounds I carry are not marks of defeat,
But of endurance,
Of a heart refined by fire
And a spirit tempered by trials.

I do not tremble,
Though the way ahead is uncertain,
For You, O God, are my confidence.
You have whispered my name in the secret place,

Called me forth from the shadows,
And placed me in the light of Your purpose.

Who am I to doubt what You have spoken?
Who am I to shrink back when Your hand is upon me?
I will walk, Lord,
In the boldness of one called by the King,
For Your Word is a lamp unto my feet,
And Your promise is a shield around my soul.

Though I am bruised,
I am not broken.
Though I have fallen,
You lift me up.
I walk with the scars of battle,
But I walk in the victory You have already won.

The world may see my frailty,
But You, O God, see my faith.
The enemy may whisper doubt,
But Your voice speaks louder still,
"Do not fear, for I am with you.
Do not be dismayed, for I am your God."

I rise with courage,
Not because I am strong,
But because You are my strength.

I press forward with boldness,
Not because I am unshaken,
But because You are my Rock.

O Lord, my confidence and my song,
I will not falter in the face of adversity,
For You have called me by name,
And Your calling does not return void.
I walk in faith,
I walk in trust,
For You are the author of my journey,
And in You, I am secure.

Bruised but bold, I stand,
A remnant woman,
Unapologetic in my calling,
Undeterred by the trials behind me,
For I know the One who walks beside me.

You, O Lord, are my confidence,
My shield, my sword, my victory.
In You, I will boldly walk,
Until every promise is fulfilled,
And Your glory is revealed through me.

# 16. Into the Wild

O Lord, You call me into the wild,
A place I do not want to go,
Where the land is barren and the path unknown,
Yet Your voice beckons me still,
Soft but certain, "Come, follow Me."

I tremble, for I know the wilderness—
A land without comfort,
A place where shadows stretch long,
Where my soul must walk alone,
Dependent only on You.
And yet, my heart hesitates,
For I am afraid of what I do not see,
Afraid of the silence,
Afraid of the storms that await me there.

O God, why must I walk this desolate road?
Can't You lead me by still waters,
And bring me to green pastures once more?
Must I face the wild winds,
The scorching sun,
The endless night?

Yet in my reluctance, I hear You whisper,

"The wild is where I shape you,
Where I strip away the fear,
And refine your faith as gold."
I am reluctant,
But I know You are true.

So, I step into the wilderness,
With trembling hands and hesitant feet,
Bruised from the battles of comfort,
But trusting in Your plan.
I walk where the ground cracks beneath me,
Where the sky is an endless expanse of uncertainty,
And I carry nothing but Your promise,
For You have said, "I will be with you,
Even in the wild."

You lead me through the desert,
Where all that I cling to is burned away.
You let the wilderness speak to my heart,
Exposing the idols I've held in secret.
The wild shows me who I am,
But more, it shows me who You are.

In this desolation, I find Your provision.
In this emptiness, I discover Your fullness.
Where once I feared hunger,
You give me manna from heaven.

Where once I feared thirst,
Your water flows from the rock.

Though I am reluctant,
You are relentless in love.
Though I walk with hesitation,
Your grace is unwavering.

Now, O God, I see the wilderness for what it is—
Not a punishment, but a preparation.
Not a curse, but a calling.
For here, in the wild, I find You closer
Than I ever did in the ease of plenty.

You are the pillar of fire by night,
The cloud that covers me by day.
Even in the wild, You are faithful.
Even in the desolation, You are my delight.

So I will walk, though my heart may tremble,
For I know that You are leading me.
Into the wild, I go,
Reluctant yet resolute,
For in this wilderness,
I will learn to trust in You alone.

O Lord, though the wild is vast,

And the journey uncertain,
I will follow You,
For You are my Guide,
My God,
My All.

# 17. The Wild Within

O Lord, You have called me to walk a path untamed,
Where the wild within me meets the wild before me.
I journey through the unknown,
A landscape rough and rugged,
But deeper still, You are refining me,
For the wilderness outside stirs the wilderness inside.

The wild within me rages at times,
Like winds that tear through barren lands,
Fears that rise like mountains unscalable,
And doubts that cast shadows over my steps.
Yet in this untamed place, You speak,
Not in the noise, but in the stillness.

O God, You know my heart—
How it wrestles, how it wars,
How it longs for peace,
Yet clings to the fight.
But You have shown me that this wildness
Is not meant to be tamed by my hand,
But surrendered to Yours.

You have called me to journey through it,
Not with chains of control,

But with the freedom of trust.
For in the wild, I learn to depend on You alone,
To walk by faith,
Not by the sight of smooth paths or clear skies.

The untamed winds blow against me,
But You, O Lord, are my shelter.
The wild within my soul seeks to break free,
But You, O Lord, are the One who brings order to chaos.
You calm the storm within me
Even as You guide me through the storm outside.

I thought the wilderness would break me,
But it has made me whole.
For in this wildness, I have found You—
Not in the safety of what I knew,
But in the surrender of the unknown.

You have taught me that the wild within
Is not something to fear,
But a place where Your strength is made perfect.
In the wilderness of my heart,
You have planted seeds of faith,
And now they bloom, even in the dry places.

O Lord, I see now that the untamed is not my enemy,
But my teacher.

For the wild within me mirrors the wildness of Your
grace,
Boundless, uncontainable,
Stretching beyond my understanding.

I walk this untamed path,
Not as one lost,
But as one found in Your purpose.
For every step through the wild within
Is a step closer to You,
And every bruise,
Every scar,
Is a testament to Your faithfulness.

Though I may not tame the wild,
I will walk boldly through it.
For You, O God, have called me
To journey through the untamed,
With courage in my heart
And faith in Your name.

The wild within me bows to You,
As does the wild before me.
And I will trust You in the untamed places,
For You are my guide,
My strength,
My peace in the wilderness.

# 18. Keys to the Wild

O Lord, You have led me into the wild,
A place I once feared,
But now I stand unshackled,
For You have placed a key in my hand.
You whispered to me, "I give you the keys of the kingdom,"
And suddenly, the wilderness no longer seemed desolate,
But full of promise, full of life.

Here in the wild, I am free.
Not bound by the expectations of man,
Nor the chains of the past,
But free to roam where Your Spirit leads,
For You have unlocked the gates
That once kept me bound in fear.

The wild no longer threatens me,
For You have given me authority,
The power to bind and to loose,
To call forth freedom even in the barren places.
What was once a wasteland
Now blooms with possibility,
For You, O Lord, have handed me the key
To unlock what the world said was lost.

In the wild, I discover the power of Your name,
The authority of Your Word.
I speak, and the earth shifts beneath my feet,
For You have made me a daughter of the King,
And the wilderness bows to Your sovereignty.

No longer do I wander aimlessly,
For You have given me direction.
With the key You placed in my hand,
I unlock the doors to freedom,
I break the chains of old burdens,
And I walk in the fullness of Your promise.

What once seemed like desolation
Is now my place of dominion.
The wild has become my sanctuary,
For in its vastness, I find You,
Closer than ever before.

You are the wind that guides me,
The flame that goes before me.
In the wilderness, I am not lost,
For You have shown me the way,
And the key to the wild
Is the authority You have granted me.

I speak life where death once reigned,
I speak peace where chaos once thrived.
For You, O Lord, have given me the power
To bind what holds me back
And loose what sets me free.

The wild is no longer my enemy,
But my inheritance.
I walk boldly through its open expanse,
For You have given me the key
That unlocks every door,
And Your promises are my guide.

Here in the wild, I am free.
Free to trust You,
Free to follow You,
Free to proclaim Your name
In the midst of the wilderness.
And with every step, I know
That You, O God,
Have already secured the victory.

The key to the wild is in my hand,
And with it, I walk boldly,
For You, O Lord, have set me free.
I will not fear the wild,

For it is where I find my freedom
In You.

# 19. Out of the Cave

O Lord, You have called me out of the cave,
Out of the darkness where I once lay buried,
Wrapped in the weight of my wounds,
Hidden from the light of Your face.
But You, O God, have spoken my name,
And at Your word, I rise.

Out of the cave I come,
Like Lazarus called from the grave,
Shaking off the dust of death,
Loosed from the bonds of despair.
For Your voice has pierced the silence,
And Your light has broken through the shadows.

The cave was my shelter once,
A place to hide from the world's sharp edges,
But it became my tomb,
A place where dreams died
And hope grew faint.
Yet in the deepest night, You found me,
And Your mercy became my morning.

O God, You breathed life into these dry bones,
And with trembling steps, I walk once more.

No longer bound by the chains of shame,
No longer silenced by the weight of sorrow.
For You have called me out of hiding,
And into the light of Your promise.

Out of the cave, I rise,
Not by my strength, but by Your grace.
Where death once reigned,
Now life springs forth,
For You, O Lord, have spoken,
And Your word does not return void.

The cave is empty now,
A memory of what was,
But no longer a prison for what is to come.
You have set my feet on solid ground,
And though I bear the scars of battle,
They testify to Your faithfulness.

I walk in the light of resurrection,
Clothed in the garments of praise.
The grave clothes are left behind,
For I am no longer bound by the past.
You have rolled away the stone,
And opened the door to my destiny.

Out of the cave, I emerge,

A remnant woman,
Restored, redeemed, renewed.
For Your love has brought me back to life,
And Your power has made me whole.

O Lord, I will not return to the shadows,
I will not retreat into fear.
For You have given me life,
And life abundant.
Out of the cave, I walk,
Into the fullness of Your light,
Into the calling You have ordained.

You are my resurrection and my life,
The One who makes all things new.
And because You have called me out of the cave,
I will live for Your glory,
Forever and always.

# 20. Victory Cry

O my King, my heart exalts in You,
For You have lifted me from the depths,
And set me high upon the rock of Your salvation.
You are my strength and my shield,
The song upon my lips,
My victory cry in the battle.

O Lord, You are mighty in power,
Clothed in majesty and splendor.
Your voice thunders over the waters,
Your word shatters the enemy's strongholds.
Who can stand against You, O King of glory?
For at the mention of Your name,
Nations tremble,
And darkness flees.

You have fought for me, O Lord,
With a sword of truth in Your hand,
And with a shield of faith, You covered me.
When my strength failed,
You were my refuge,
When the arrows flew,
You were my defense.
By Your hand, O God,

The battle was won before I ever stood to fight.

I lift my hands in praise to You,
For You have crowned me with Your victory.
The scars I bear are now my testimony,
The wounds I carried now shine with Your healing.
What was once broken, You have made whole,
What was lost, You have redeemed.

O King, Your faithfulness is my song,
Your mercy my anthem.
Though I walked through the valley of despair,
You, O Lord, led me through the darkness,
Your light guiding every step.
You did not forsake me,
Even when I faltered,
But with love unfailing,
You called me by name.

Let the heavens declare Your glory,
Let the earth proclaim Your praise!
For You alone, O God, are worthy,
Worthy of every hallelujah.
Your kingdom reigns forever,
And Your righteousness endures through all generations.

You are my banner,

The standard raised high over my life.
In Your name, I find my courage,
In Your promise, I find my rest.
No weapon formed against me shall prosper,
For You have already claimed the victory.

With my heart, I cry out to You, O King,
For You are my Deliverer,
My Savior,
My Redeemer.
You have turned my mourning into dancing,
And clothed me in garments of praise.

Forever will I sing of Your greatness,
Forever will I proclaim Your name.
For You have written Your law upon my heart,
And Your Spirit has sealed me with Your love.
I am Yours, O Lord,
And You are my King,
Forever and always.

Let every breath be a victory cry,
For You have triumphed over all!
You are the King of kings,
The Lord of lords,
And Your reign is everlasting.

Victory belongs to You, O God,
And I, Your remnant,
Shall declare it
From the depths of my soul,
Forever.

# 21. Song of the Unshaken

O Lord, how mighty is the woman who stands,
Rooted in the rock of Your truth,
Her heart steadfast, her gaze unyielding,
For she knows the One in whom she trusts.
Though the storms rage and the winds howl,
She is unmoved, unshaken by the fury,
For her faith is anchored in Your Word,
And her soul rests in the shadow of Your wings.

Many have risen against her,
Voices loud with doubt and disdain,
Yet she does not bow to the fear of man,
For her fear is only of You, O Lord.
In the midst of the battle, she stands tall,
Clad in the armor of Your righteousness,
Shielded by the truth You have spoken,
Holding the sword of Your Spirit in her hand.

They said she would falter,
That her path was too hard to walk,
But she walks in the footsteps of her Savior,
Who has already gone before her.
Her faith is her shield,
Her hope a bright flame that cannot be quenched.

Even in the valley of shadow,
She sings songs of victory,
For she knows the battle is already won.

O Lord, You are her strength and her song,
And in You, she finds her refuge.
Though the world may rise against her,
Her confidence remains unshaken,
For her heart is hidden in Your promises,
And her eyes are fixed upon Your face.

When the waves of opposition crash upon her,
She stands firm upon the shore,
Knowing that her foundation cannot be moved,
For You, O God, are the rock beneath her feet.
Her faith is not in what she sees,
But in the unseen power of Your hand,
And she will not be swayed by the winds of doubt.

O remnant woman, stand strong in the Lord,
For He is your fortress,
Your deliverer in times of trouble.
Your enemies may surround you,
But they will not prevail,
For the Lord of Hosts is with you,
And His love is your shield.

Lift up your head, O daughter of Zion,
For your King has called you by name.
Walk in the boldness of His promises,
And let your unwavering faith be a banner
That speaks of His goodness,
A testament to His grace.

You are not forsaken,
Nor will you ever be alone,
For the God who formed you
Is the God who fights for you.
And in His strength, you will stand forever,
Unmoved, unbroken,
A remnant of His faithfulness in the earth.